A Viola Advent

25 Days of Christmas Solos and Duets for a Most Joyous Season

Book One   Myanna Harvey and Cassia Harvey

Cover Image
The Miriam and Ira D. Wallach Division of Art, Prints and Photographs: Picture Collection, The New York Public Library. "Christmas greetings." The New York Public Library Digital Collections. https://digitalcollections.nypl.org/items/510d47e3-6f8c-a3d9-e040-e00a18064a99

CHP432

©2022 C. Harvey Publications®
All Rights Reserved.
www.charveypublications.com - print books
www.learnstrings.com - downloadable books
www.harveystringarrangements.com - chamber music

Table of Contents

                          Page

How the Book Works	3
Dec. 1: The First Noel	4
Dec. 2: We Three Kings	6
Dec. 3: Good King Wenceslas	8
Dec. 4: Go, Tell It on the Mountain	10
Dec. 5: Jingle Bells	12
Dec. 6: O Come, All Ye Faithful	16
Dec. 7: Away in a Manger	18
Dec. 8: O Christmas Tree	20
Dec. 9: Angels We Have Heard on High	22
Dec. 10: Up on the Housetop	26
Dec. 11: God Rest Ye, Merry Gentlemen	28
Dec. 12: O Little Town of Bethlehem	30
Dec. 13: I Saw Three Ships	32
Dec. 14: March from **The Nutcracker**	34
Dec. 15: What Child is This	38
Dec. 16: O Holy Night	42
Dec. 17: O Come, O Come Emmanuel	46
Dec. 18: The Twelve Days of Christmas	48
Dec. 19: Carol of the Bells	52
Dec. 20: Deck the Halls	54
Dec. 21: Hark, the Herald Angels Sing	56
Dec. 22: Waltz from **The Nutcracker**	58
Dec. 23: Joy to the World	62
Dec. 24: Silent Night	64
Dec. 25: We Wish You a Merry Christmas	66

How the Book Works

This book can work as a music advent calendar, giving you warm-up exercises, melodies, and variations on carols to play on the days leading up to Christmas.

On each day of December, you can play a warm-up, then the melody, and finally work on the variation. Then, you can play the melodies and variations with viola duet parts at a lesson or a chamber music session.

Looking to play Christmas music with friends? This book is compatible with the Violin and the Cello books and can be used to play Christmas duets with those instruments as well!

Play-Along Files

Links to available play-along files and videos can be found at www.charveypublications.com/adventplayalong.

Performance Suggestion

When performing from the book, a good way to format a carol would be to play the Melody, the Variation, and then the Melody again.

Please note: Playing the Melody simultaneously with another player playing the Variation is not recommended.

Free Sheet Music from C. Harvey Publications!

Free exercises, solos, and duets can be found on our blog at https://www.charveypublications.com/better-string-playing-blog

Have a Question?

We are here to answer questions about the book! Email us at charveypublications@gmail.com or fill out the contact form here: https://www.charveypublications.com/contact.html

©2022 C. Harvey Publications® All Rights Reserved.

December 1st: Warm-Up for The First Noel

C. Harvey

December 1st Melody: The First Noel

Traditional French Carol

A Viola Advent, Book One

December 1st Variation: The First Noel

M. Harvey, after Traditional Melody

December 1st Duet Part: The First Noel

M. Harvey

©2022 C. Harvey Publications All Rights Reserved.

December 2nd: Warm-Up for We Three Kings

C. Harvey

Tremolo: In the upper half of the bow, move the bow back and forth very lightly, and as fast as possible for the length of the note.

December 2nd Melody: We Three Kings

J. Hopkins

©2022 C. Harvey Publications All Rights Reserved.

December 3rd: Warm-Up for Good King Wenceslas

C. Harvey

December 3rd Melody: Good King Wenceslas

Piae Cantones, arr. J. Stainer

A Viola Advent, Book One 9

December 3rd Variation: Good King Wenceslas

M. Harvey, after Piao Cantones

December 3rd Duet Part: Good King Wenceslas

M. Harvey

©2022 C. Harvey Publications All Rights Reserved.

A Viola Advent, Book One

11

December 4th Variation: Go, Tell It On the Mountain

Moderato

M. Harvey, after Traditional Spiritual

December 4th Duet Part: Go, Tell It On the Mountain

Moderato

M. Harvey

©2022 C. Harvey Publications All Rights Reserved.

December 5th: Warm-Ups for Jingle Bells

G Major Scale

C. Harvey

G Major Etude

C. Harvey

Agility Etude

C. Harvey

14

A Viola Advent, Book One

December 5th Melody: Jingle Bells

J. Pierpont

Allegro

December 5th Variation: Jingle Bells

M. Harvey, after J. Pierpont

Allegro

©2022 C. Harvey Publications All Rights Reserved.

A Viola Advent, Book One

December 5th Duet Part: Jingle Bells

M. Harvey

Allegro

December 6th: Warm-Up for O Come, All Ye Faithful

C. Harvey

December 6th Melody: O Come, All Ye Faithful

Moderato

J. Wade

©2022 C. Harvey Publications All Rights Reserved.

December 7th: Warm-Up for Away in a Manger

C. Harvey

December 7th Melody: Away in a Manger

J. Murray

©2022 C. Harvey Publications All Rights Reserved.

A Viola Advent, Book One

December 7th Variation: Away in a Manger

Andante

M. Harvey, after J. Murray

December 7th Duet Part: Away in a Manger

Andante

M. Harvey

©2022 C. Harvey Publications All Rights Reserved.

December 8th: Warm-Up for O Christmas Tree

C. Harvey

December 8th Melody: O Christmas Tree

Moderato

Traditional Melody

©2022 C. Harvey Publications All Rights Reserved.

December 9th: Warm-Ups for Angels We Have Heard on High

C. Harvey

D Major Scale Etude

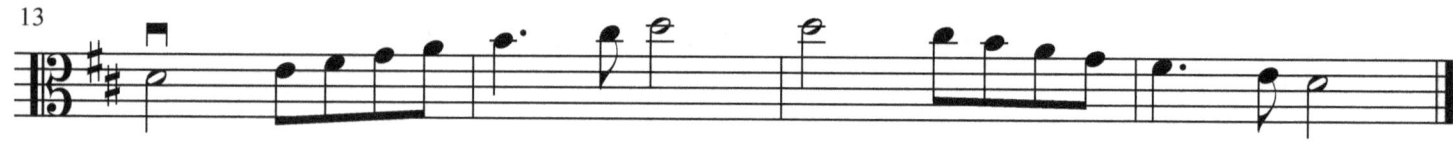

Mordent

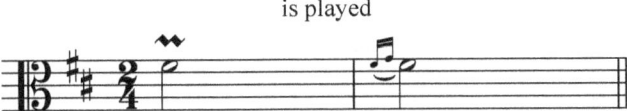
is played

String Crossing Etude

C. Harvey

December 9th Melody: Angels We Have Heard on High

Traditional Melody

December 9th Variation: Angels We Have Heard on High

M. Harvey, after Trad. Melody

A Viola Advent, Book One

25

December 9th Duet Part: Angels We Have Heard on High

M. Harvey

©2022 C. Harvey Publications All Rights Reserved.

December 10th: Warm-Up for Up on the Housetop

C. Harvey

Left-hand pizzicato

December 10th Melody: Up on the Housetop

B. Hanby

Allegro

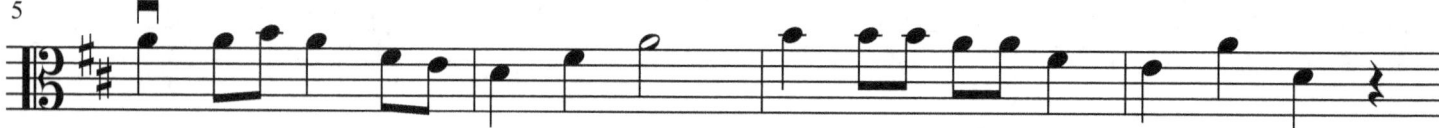

©2022 C. Harvey Publications All Rights Reserved.

A Viola Advent, Book One

27

December 10th Variation: Up on the Housetop

M. Harvey, after B. Hanby

December 10th Duet Part: Up on the Housetop

M. Harvey

©2022 C. Harvey Publications All Rights Reserved.

December 11th: Warm-Up for God Rest Ye, Merry Gentlemen

C. Harvey

December 11th Melody: God Rest Ye, Merry Gentlemen

Traditional Melody

A Viola Advent, Book One
29

December 11th Variation: God Rest Ye, Merry Gentlemen

Moderato

M. Harvey, after Traditional Melody

December 11th Duet Part: God Rest Ye, Merry Gentlemen

Moderato

M. Harvey

©2022 C. Harvey Publications All Rights Reserved.

December 12th: Warm-Up for O Little Town of Bethlehem

C. Harvey

December 12th Melody: O Little Town of Bethlehem

L. Redner

Andante

A Viola Advent, Book One

December 12th Variation: O Little Town of Bethlehem

M. Harvey, after L. Redner

December 12th Duet Part: O Little Town of Bethlehem

M. Harvey

©2022 C. Harvey Publications All Rights Reserved.

December 13th: Warm-Up for I Saw Three Ships

C. Harvey

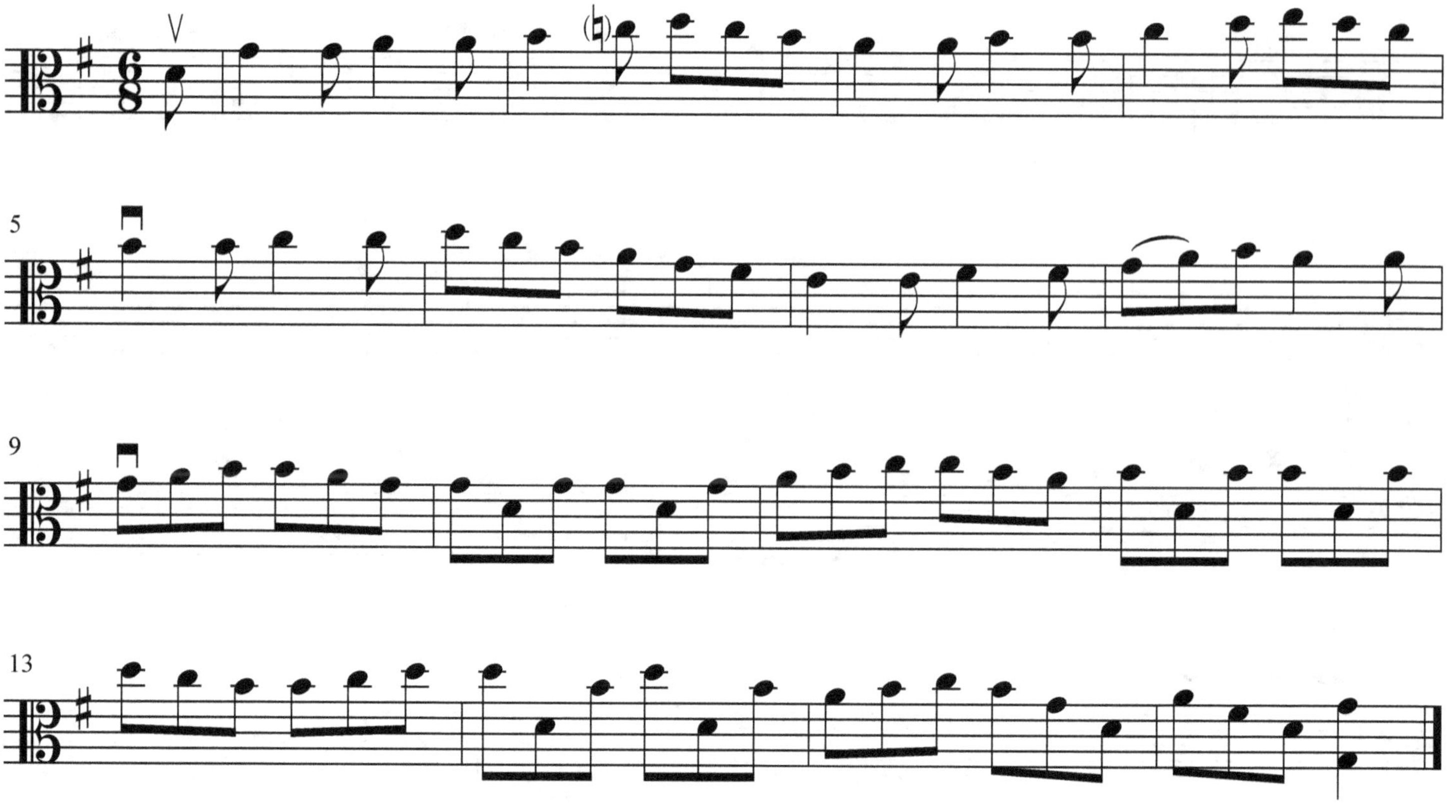

December 13th Melody: I Saw Three Ships

Traditional Melody

Vivace

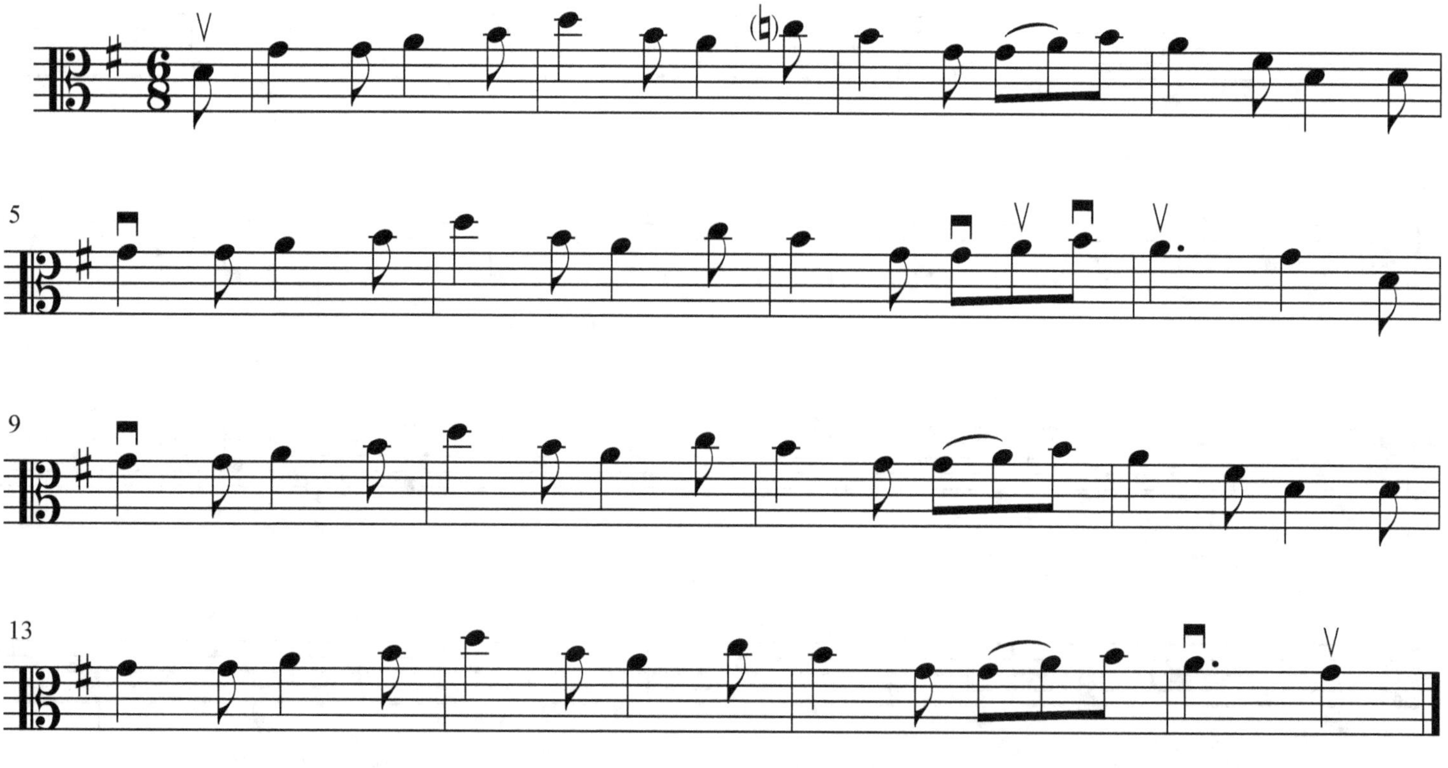

A Viola Advent, Book One 33

December 13th Variation: I Saw Three Ships

M. Harvey, after Traditional Melody

December 13th Duet Part: I Saw Three Ships

M. Harvey

©2022 C. Harvey Publications All Rights Reserved.

December 14th: Warm-Ups for March from *The Nutcracker*

D Major Scale Rhythm No. 1

C. Harvey

D Major Scale Rhythm No. 2

C. Harvey

D Major Rhythm Etude

C. Harvey

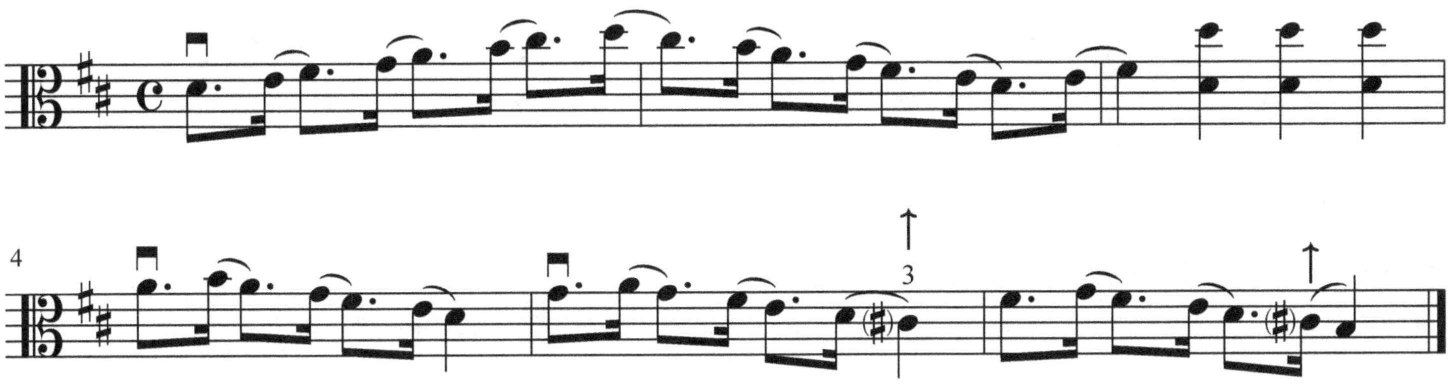

C♯ and A♯

C. Harvey

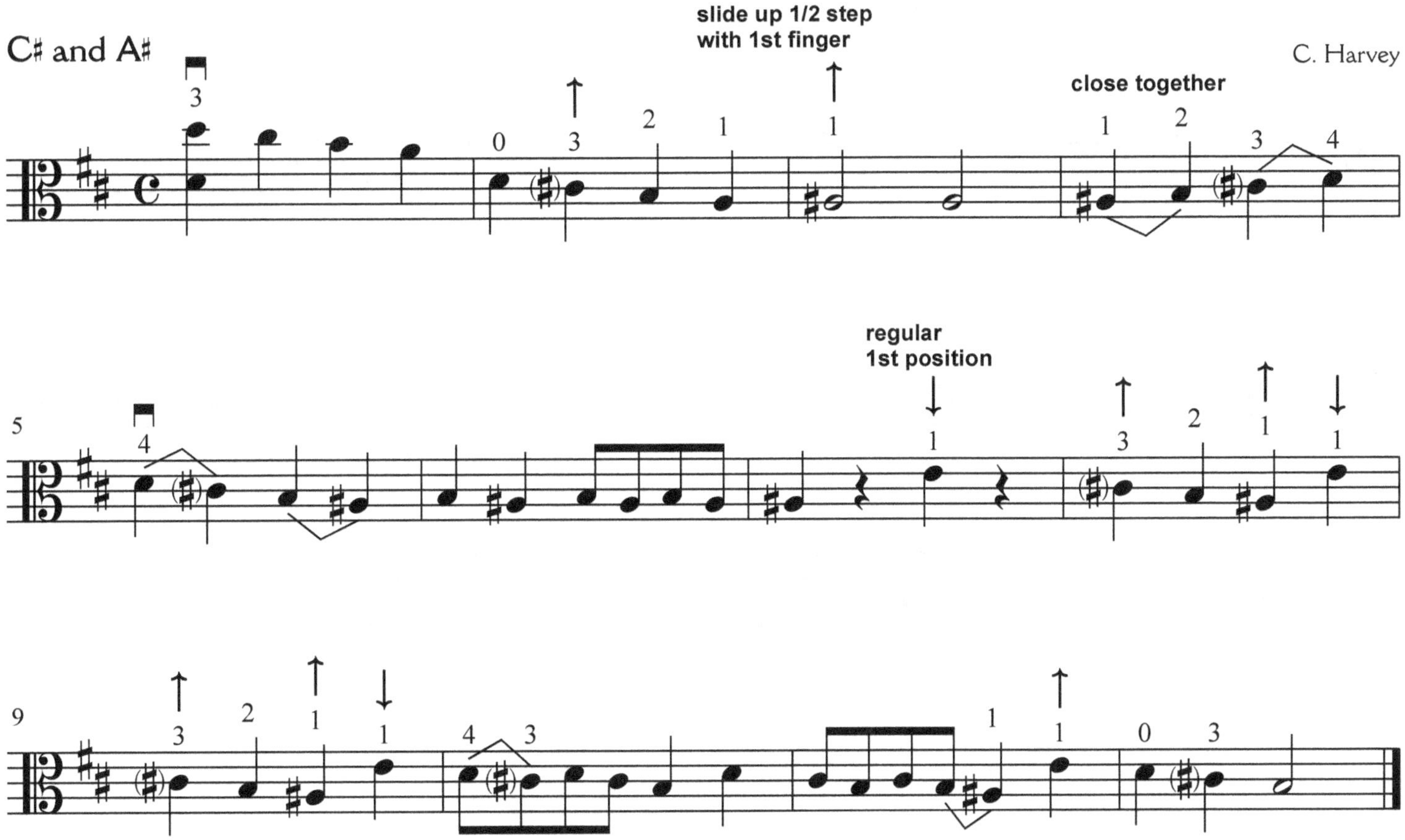

slide up 1/2 step with 1st finger

close together

regular 1st position

December 14th Melody: March from *The Nutcracker*

P. Tchaikovsky

A Viola Advent, Book One

December 14th Variation: March from *The Nutcracker*

Tempo di Marcia

P. Tchaikovsky, arr. M. Harvey

December 14th Duet Part: March from *The Nutcracker*

Tempo di Marcia

M. Harvey, after P. Tchaikovsky

©2022 C. Harvey Publications All Rights Reserved.

December 15th: Warm-Ups for What Child Is This

D Minor Etude No. 1

C. Harvey

D Minor Etude No. 2

C. Harvey

December 15th Melody: What Child Is This

Moderato

Traditional Melody

December 15th Variation: What Child Is This

Moderato

M. Harvey, after Traditional Melody

©2022 C. Harvey Publications All Rights Reserved.

December 16th: Warm-Ups for O Holy Night

C Major Etude No. 1

C. Harvey

C Major Etude No. 2

C. Harvey

December 16th Melody: O Holy Night

Andante

A. Adam

December 16th Variation: O Holy Night

M. Harvey, after A. Adam

Andante

©2022 C. Harvey Publications All Rights Reserved.

A Viola Advent, Book One

December 16th Duet Part: O Holy Night

M. Harvey

December 17th: Warm-Up for O Come, O Come Emmanuel

C. Harvey

December 17th Melody: O Come, O Come Emmanuel

Plainsong

December 18th: Warm-Ups for The Twelve Days of Christmas

Twelve Days Bow Rhythm Etude

C. Harvey

Twelve Days Agility Etude

C. Harvey

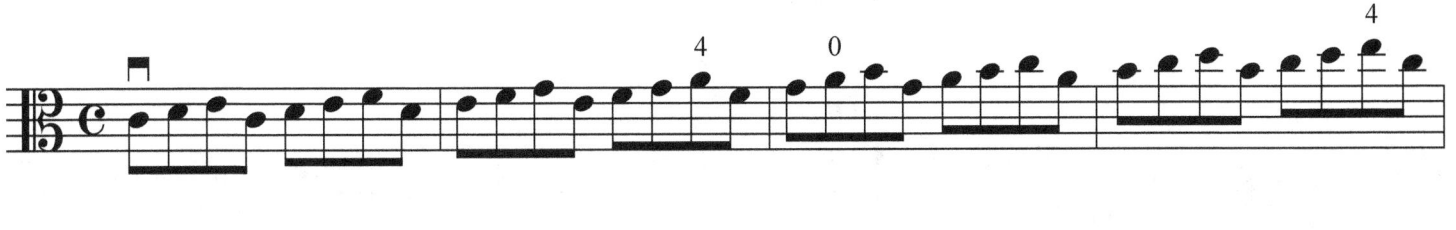
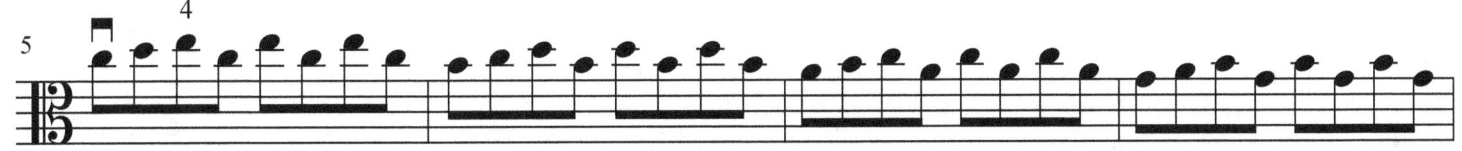

December 18th Melody: The Twelve Days of Christmas

Allegro

Traditional Melody

December 18th Variation: The Twelve Days of Christmas

M. Harvey, after Traditional Melody

Allegro

A Viola Advent, Book One

December 18th Duet Part: The Twelve Days of Christmas

M. Harvey

Allegro

December 19th: Warm-Up for Carol of the Bells

C. Harvey

December 19th Melody: Carol of the Bells

M. Leontovych

Allegro

©2022 C. Harvey Publications All Rights Reserved.

A Viola Advent, Book One

December 19th Variation: Carol of the Bells

M. Harvey, after M. Leontovych

December 19th Duet Part: Carol of the Bells

M. Harvey

©2022 C. Harvey Publications All Rights Reserved.

December 20th: Warm-Up for Deck the Halls

C. Harvey

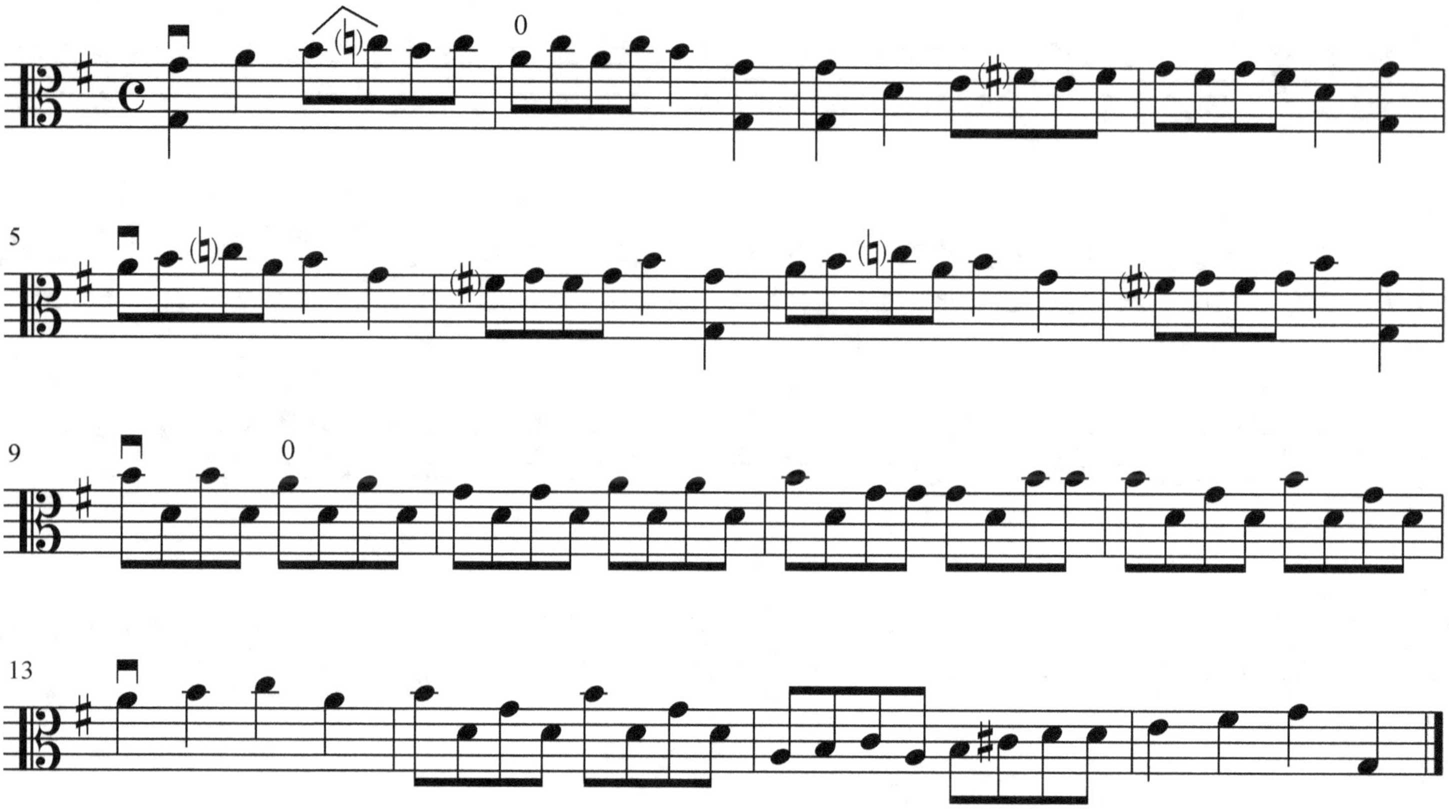

December 20th Melody: Deck the Halls

Allegro

T. Oliphant

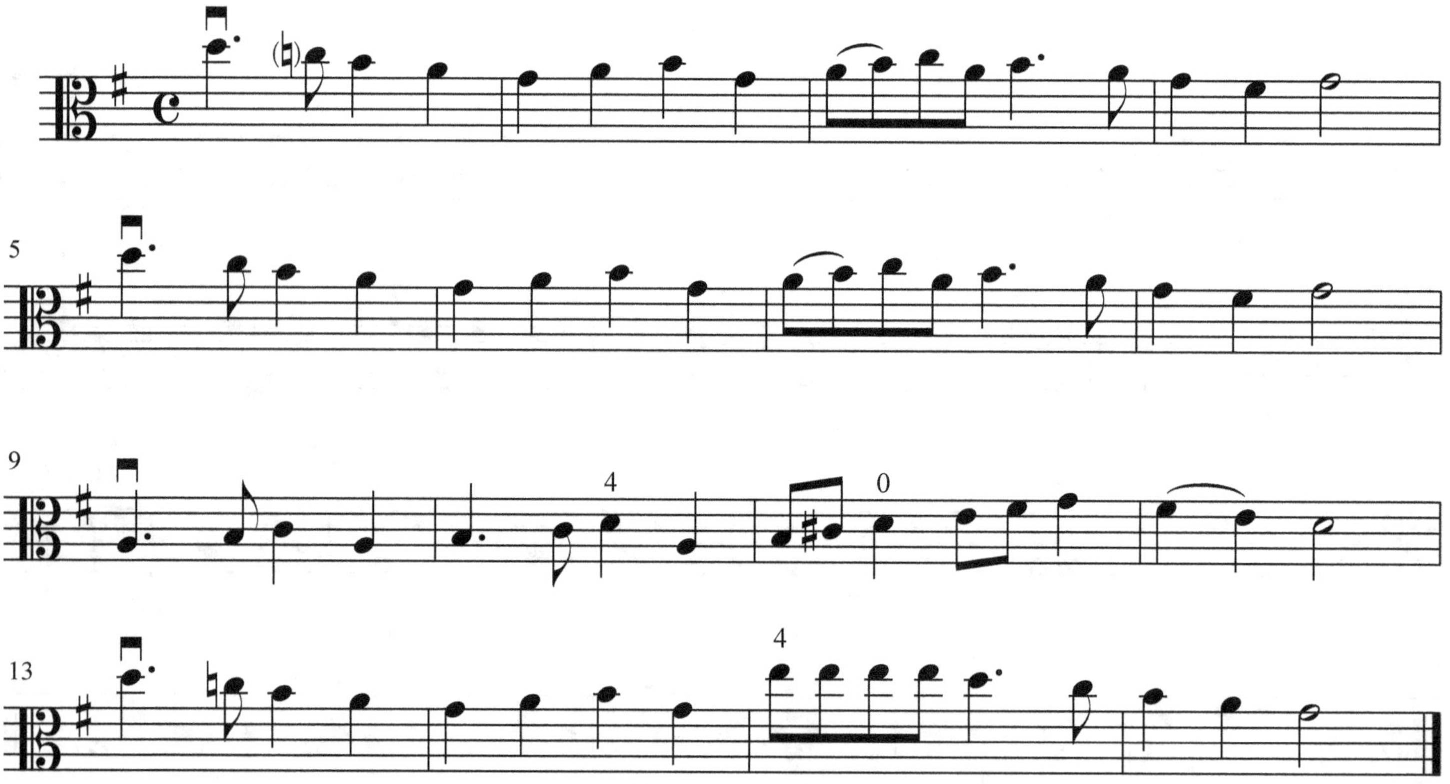

A Viola Advent, Book One
55

December 20th Variation: Deck the Halls

M. Harvey, after T. Oliphant

December 20th Duet Part: Deck the Halls

M. Harvey

©2022 C. Harvey Publications All Rights Reserved.

December 21st: Warm-Up for Hark, the Herald Angels Sing

C. Harvey

December 21st Melody: Hark, the Herald Angels Sing

F. Mendelssohn

Moderato

A Viola Advent, Book One

December 21st Variation: Hark, the Herald Angels Sing

M. Harvey, after F. Mendelssohn

December 21st Duet Part: Hark, the Herald Angels Sing

M. Harvey

©2022 C. Harvey Publications All Rights Reserved.

December 22nd: Warm-Ups for Waltz from *The Nutcracker*

G# Study

C. Harvey

E♯ Study
C. Harvey

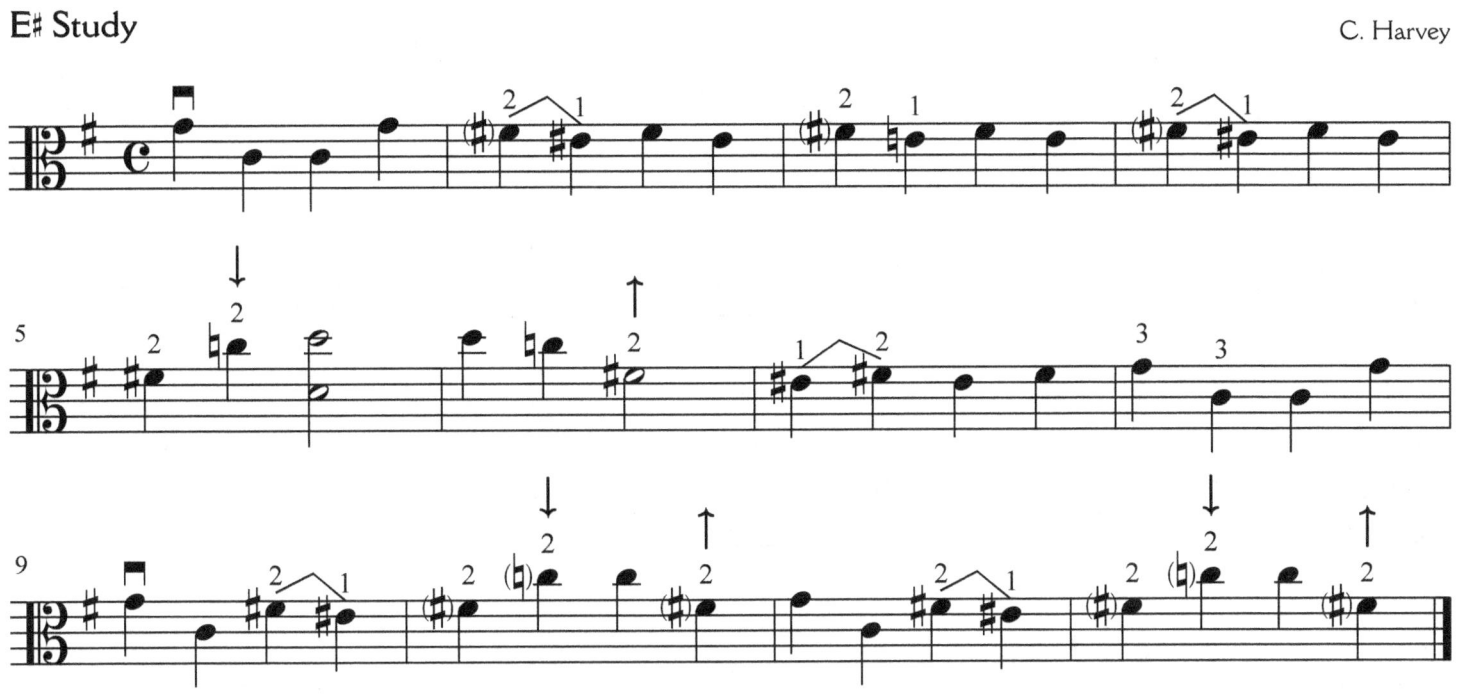

Scale Rhythm Study
C. Harvey

December 22nd Melody: Waltz of the Flowers, from *The Nutcracker*

P. Tchaikovsky

December 22nd Variation: Waltz of the Flowers, from *The Nutcracker*

P. Tchaikovsky, arr. M. Harvey

©2022 C. Harvey Publications All Rights Reserved.

A Viola Advent, Book One

61

December 22nd Duet Part: Waltz of the Flowers, from *The Nutcracker*

M. Harvey, after P. Tchaikovsky

Tempo di Valse

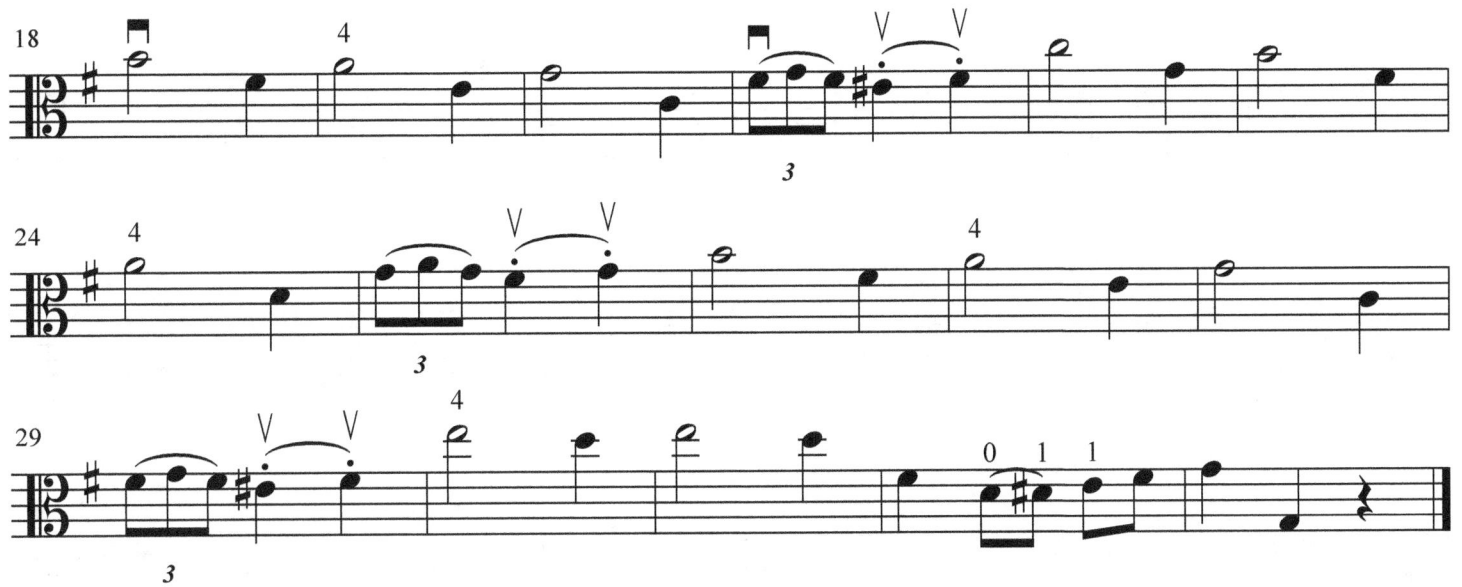

©2022 C. Harvey Publications All Rights Reserved.

A Viola Advent, Book One

December 23rd Variation: Joy To the World

M. Harvey, after L. Mason

December 23rd Duet Part: Joy To the World

M. Harvey

©2022 C. Harvey Publications All Rights Reserved.

December 24th: Warm-Up for Silent Night

December 24th Melody: Silent Night

A Viola Advent, Book One

December 24th Variation: Silent Night

M. Harvey, after F. Gruber

December 24th Duet Part: Silent Night

M. Harvey

©2022 C. Harvey Publications All Rights Reserved.

December 25th: Warm-Up for We Wish You a Merry Christmas

C. Harvey

December 25th Melody: We Wish You a Merry Christmas

Vivace

Traditional Melody

A Viola Advent, Book One

December 25th Variation: We Wish You a Merry Christmas

M. Harvey, after Traditional Melody

December 25th Duet Part: We Wish You a Merry Christmas

M. Harvey

©2022 C. Harvey Publications All Rights Reserved.

Available from www.charveypublications.com
The Blackberry Blossom Fiddle Book for Viola CHP384

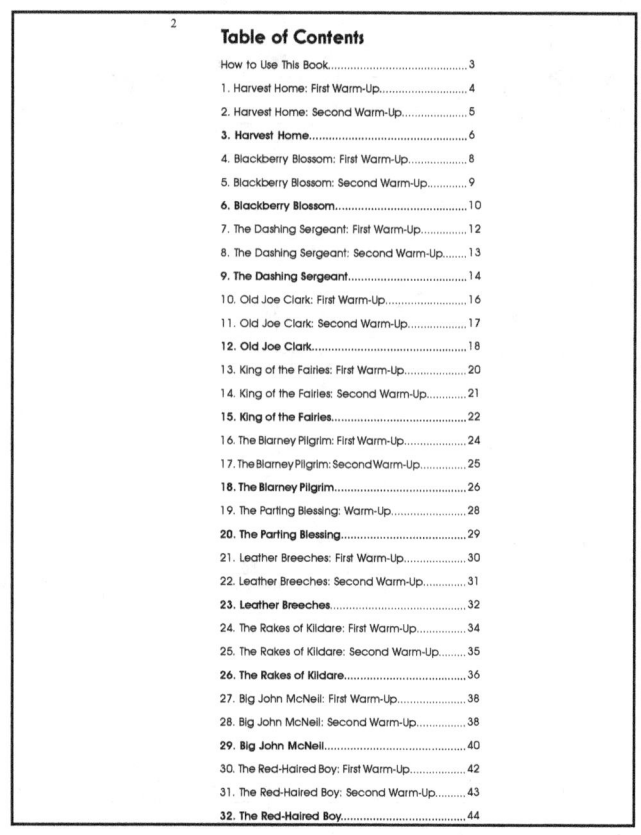

Fiddle Exercises at two different levels.

Fiddle Tunes at two different levels can be played solo, in duets, or in chamber ensembles.

Exercises, Tunes, and Harmonies are compatible with the violin, cello, and string bass books!